To Alan + Denny —
Great natural beauty!
Howard + Lili

THE

ROCKIES

CANADA'S MAGNIFICENT WILDERNESS

THE
ROCKIES
CANADA'S MAGNIFICENT WILDERNESS

Photography by
PAUL LALLY & JOHN WINNIE
Text by
BEN GADD

Beautiful America Publishing Company

Published by
Beautiful America Publishing Company©
P.O. Box 646
Wilsonville, Oregon 97070

Design: Jacelen Pete
Editing: Andrea Tronslin
Linotronic Output: LeFont Laser Imaging and Design

Library of Congress Cataloging-in-Publication Data

Winnie, John. 1959-
        The Rockies: Canada's magnificent wilderness/
photography by John Winnie & Paul Lally: written by Ben Gadd.
        p. cm.
ISBN 0-89802-588-5: $24.95
        1. Canadian Rockies (B.C. and Alta.)--Description and
travel-Views. 2. Natural history--Canadian Rockies (B.C. and Alta.)
-Pictorial words. I. Lally, Paul, 1956- . II. Gadd, Ben, 1946-
F1090.W75 1992
508.711--dc20   91-40024
                                                                         CIP

To all those who open their eyes to the beauty of nature,
and their hearts to its preservation.

Map of the Canadian Rockies

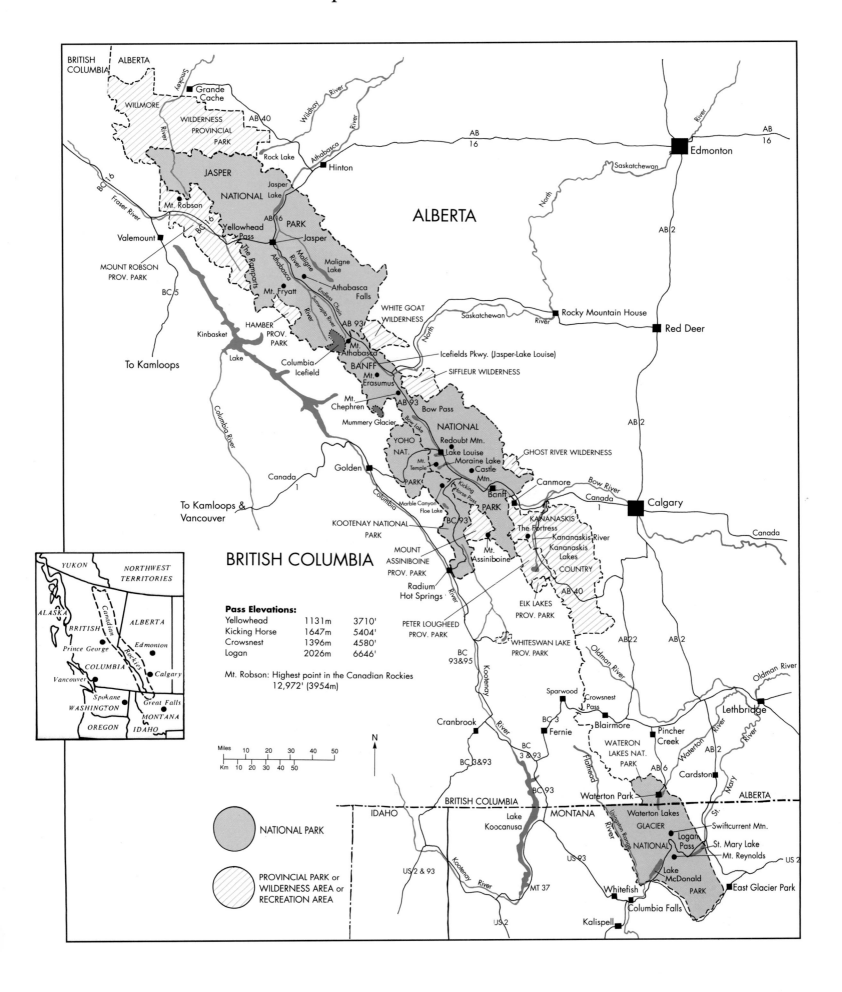

BRITISH COLUMBIA

ALBERTA

Smoky River

Grande Cache

WILLMORE

WILDERNESS PROVINCIAL PARK

AB 40

Wildhay River

River

AB 16

AB 16

Edmonton

Rock Lake

Athabasca River

Hinton

Saskatchewan

BC 16

JASPER

Jasper Lake

Fraser River

Mt. Robson

NATIONAL

ALBERTA

BC 16

Yellowhead Pass

AB 16

PARK

Jasper

AB 2

Valemount

MOUNT ROBSON PROV. PARK

The Ramparts

Athabasca River

Maligne River

Maligne Lake

BC 5

Mt. Fryatt

Athabasca Falls

Endless Chain

Sunwapta River

WHITE GOAT WILDERNESS

North

Saskatchewan

River

Rocky Mountain House

Red Deer

Kinbasket

HAMBER PROV. PARK

AB 93

To Kamloops

Columbia River

Lake

Columbia Icefield

Mt. Athabasca

Icefields Pkwy. (Jasper-Lake Louise)

SIFFLEUR WILDERNESS

BANFF

Mt. Erasumus

AB 93

Mt. Chephren

Bow Pass

AB 2

Canada 1

Golden

Mummery Glacier

Bow Lake

NATIONAL

Redoubt Mtn.

GHOST RIVER WILDERNESS

To Kamloops & Vancouver

YOHO NAT. PARK

Mt. Temple

Lake Louise

Moraine Lake

Castle Mtn.

Kicking Horse Pass

Canmore

Bow River

Calgary

Columbia River

Marble Canyon

Floe Lake

BC 93

Banff

PARK

KANANASKIS

The Fortress

Kananaskis River

Canada 1

Canada

KOOTENAY NATIONAL PARK

MOUNT ASSINIBOINE PROV. PARK

Mt. Assiniboine

Kananaskis Lakes

COUNTRY

Radium Hot Springs

AB 40

BRITISH COLUMBIA

ELK LAKES PROV. PARK

Pass Elevations:

Yellowhead	1131m	3710'
Kicking Horse	1647m	5404'
Crowsnest	1396m	4580'
Logan	2026m	6646'

PETER LOUGHEED PROV. PARK

AB 22

AB 2

Mt. Robson: Highest point in the Canadian Rockies 12,972' (3954m)

WHITESWAN LAKE PROV. PARK

Oldman River

Oldman River

Kootenay River

BC 93&95

Sparwood

Crowsnest Pass

Lethbridge

Cranbrook

BC 3

Fernie

Blairmore

Pincher Creek

AB 2

BC 3 &93

WATERON LAKES NAT. PARK

AB 6

Cardston

Waterton River

Mary

BC 3&93

Flathead River

Waterton Park

Waterton Lakes

ALBERTA

BC 93

Livingston Range

GLACIER

Swiftcurrent Mtn.

St. Mary Lake

BRITISH COLUMBIA

IDAHO

Lake Koocanusa

MONTANA

Logan Pass

NATIONAL

Mt. Reynolds

US 2

Miles 10 20 30 40 50

Km 10 20 30 40 50

N

US 93

Lake McDonald

Whitefish

PARK

East Glacier Park

NATIONAL PARK

PROVINCIAL PARK or WILDERNESS AREA or RECREATION AREA

US 2 & 93

Kootenay River

MT 37

Columbia Falls

Kalispell

US 2

Inset map

YUKON

NORTHWEST TERRITORIES

ALASKA

BRITISH

Canadian Rockies

ALBERTA

Prince George

Edmonton

COLUMBIA

Calgary

Vancouver

Spokane

Great Falls

WASHINGTON

MONTANA

OREGON

IDAHO

Introduction

Ah, the Canadian Rockies. Just like Switzerland, and a lot closer to home. Right?

Well, yes and no.

Yes, the Canadian Rockies look a lot like the Swiss Alps—especially the Alps around Zermatt, under the Matterhorn. In the Rockies near Banff lies Mount Assiniboine, a peak in the same class. The Alps have glaciers; the Rockies have glaciers. The Alps have enormous cliffs and so do the Rockies.

But no, the Rockies don't have the granite spires of Chamonix. And the summit of the Matterhorn is higher than the summit of Mt. Assiniboine.

Other things are missing from the Canadian Rockies: yodelling milkmaids, for example (these are also in short supply in Switzerland, I'm told), and watch factories, and cog trains creeping up the peaks. Very few cows gobble the grass in Canadian alpine meadows, and hardly any thickets of chalets cling to the slopes.

Gosh. Maybe that isn't so bad.

In fact, it's terrifically good. Switzerland is overwhelmed with humanity year-round, and Canada is not. The Canadian Rockies get overwhelmed only in the tourist towns of Jasper and Banff, and only in July and August. If you were to parachute randomly into the Canadian Rockies, you would have to make hundreds of drops before you landed in sight of anyone at all. The people of Switzerland are delighted with that; they come *here* on their vacations—although they seldom ask to go parachuting.

This is all by way of introducing the format of this book. In it you will find pictures of mountains, pictures of lakes, pictures of rivers, pictures of wildflowers, pictures of birds and bears—111 pictures in total, all of them great photographs of classic Canadian Rockies subjects, and *none of them has a human being in it.*

The photographers, Paul Lally and John Winnie, wanted it that way. Their reason was simple. By and large, that's how the Canadian Rockies are: unpeopled. In an age of overpopulation and environmental messes, the Canadian Rockies are still mostly unspoiled. They are still wilderness.

Paul and John could easily have taken the sort of pictures you see in so many coffeetable books about the Rockies: pictures of hotels and tramways and people riding horses on trails. That's all very nice, but it wasn't what John and Paul wanted. They wanted to photograph the *real* Rockies, the *wild* Rockies.

So they had to walk. Paul and John put on their packs—heavy packs, full of cameras and lenses, with tripods dangling—and they went to places that you won't see in those other books. In the winter they went on snowshoes and cross-country skis. They worked hard for these pictures, and it shows. I hope you enjoy them as much as I did in writing the words to go with them.

Ben Gadd, Jasper National Park
September 19, 1991

*Left: **grizzly bear** (Ursus arctos)*

Spring breakup

Sunset—and the end of another day of melt on Lake McDonald. Frozen two feet thick (half a metre) by January's arctic cold, the ice thins in March, when the sun has the power to penetrate it. The surface turns gray. The bonds linking the crystals weaken. One day there is open water; another day a steady tinkling sound announces the presence of candle ice: vertical rods that fall in as the ice edge retreats. Within a week it is over. The lake ripples again in the wind, and for the fish below the waves it couldn't have happened too soon.

Above: Waterton-Glacier International Peace Park, Montana

Sans thunderbolts,
but impressive just the same

A bald eagle on the wing is one of the grand views of the Rockies; it flies in the stately manner of an airliner. Its lifestyle, on the other hand, is not as first-class (by human standards) as might be assumed: the bird lives mainly on dead fish.

For many years, a run of kokanee trout upstream from Flathead Lake in the fall brought hundreds of eagles to the little community of Apgar, just inside the western boundary of Glacier National Park, Montana. It was the greatest gathering of bald eagles in the Rockies. But an ill-conceived introduction of exotic crustaceans into Flathead Lake by state fisheries officials did in the trout, and now the eagles at Apgar are few.

Above: bald eagle (Haliaeetus leucocephalus)

Pine forest

Well, not all of the trees shown here are pines. There are spruces as well. But most of the trees in the picture are ponderosa pines, their reddish-brown trunks looking very handsome in the snow. Ponderosa pines are sun-loving trees that survive in the Canadian Rockies only in the warmest, driest part of the region: in the Rocky Mountain Trench from Radium Hot Springs south. Elsewhere, they are replaced by the cold-adapted lodgepole pine.

*Above: **ponderosa pine** (Pinus ponderosa)*

Aftermath of a storm

It took a major weather system to produce this scene, dropping enough snow to cover everything well. The snow must have been wet, too, or it would not cling to the steep slopes the way it does, nor would it leave the trees looking as if they had been dipped in plaster. Clouds still stream from the summits, the remnants of a blizzard.

Above: alpenglow on the Livingston Range, Waterton-Glacier
International Peace Park, Montana

Right: beargrass (Xerophyllum tenax)

Oldest rock in the Rockies

Well, the oldest *sedimentary* rock: 1.5 billion years. In a few places the granite of the North American Plate is exposed, and that is older yet: about two billion years. But the red-and-green shales of Waterton-Glacier are quite ancient as sediments go; layered rock of that age is rare on this planet.

These layers are known to U.S. geologists as the Belt Group, and to Canadians as the Purcell Group. Most of this rock accumulated as mud on tidal flats along the seacoast. At that time life consisted mostly of blue-green algae (properly termed cyanobacteria) in the sea.

Were there any animals in those waters? Perhaps; but if there were, they had soft bodies that left no shells as fossils, nor did they leave any sign of their presence, such as tracks or burrows. Incredibly, though, the same sort of algal colonies prevalent in Purcell time are still present in the world today.

Beargrass ...

... is not really grass, but it *is* popular with bears—especially grizzly bears, which eat the flowerheads. The leaves are long and skinny; they make the plant look like a grass species. However, the showy bloom of *Xerophyllum tenax* shows that it is actually a lily. It grows no farther north than Crowsnest Pass, making it the unofficial symbol of the Waterton-Glacier area.

Left: in the background—Mt. Reynolds, Waterton-Glacier International Peace Park, Montana

Above: lounging nannies with kids

White boulders on the slopes—until they move

Seeing mountain goats in winter is well nigh impossible from a distance; they are white on white. In summer it's easier, when the animals stand out against dark rock or green tundra. But one usually sees them from far away (from far *below*), and at such a distance they look like pale rocks, of which there are many in the mountains. Given a candidate fixed in the binoculars, you have to wait to see if it moves.

The group pictured here is probably all nannies and kids. It's hard to tell the billies from the nannies at a distance (or even up close, their coats are so long), but here are a couple of clues: if it has a kid with it, it's going to be a nanny. If the horns slope back abruptly at the tip, it's probably a nanny. If its horns are more gently curved and it's somewhat larger than the other animals, then it's probably a billy.

The kid pictured here has a good chance of living a long life in the Canadian Rockies. Mountain goats do have predators—grizzly bears, cougars, wolves and wolverines all go after them—but none kills them regularly. The goats seldom venture far from cliffy terrain, on which they climb so well that nothing can reach them. In fact, the major causes of death among mountain goats are falling and being caught in snowslides. As long as this youngster watches where it goes on steep rock and snow, it could live to be 10 or 15 years old.

Above: bighorn sheep, Waterton-Glacier International Peace Park, Montana

Alpine favorite

While picking his way through this hostile-looking terrain, the photographer was surprised—as so many people are—to see such a cheery-looking plant blooming among the rocks. But that's typical of moss campion (*Silene acaulis*), a much-loved alpine wildflower. Starting from a few tiny, moss-like leaves, moss campion gradually builds a big cushiony colony over the stones. Thus it is a tundra producer.

Wildflowers in the alpine zone have only a couple of months each year to grow and produce seed. In consideration of that, high-country hikers must be careful not to tread on these pretty cushions. A big one like this could be two hundred years old.

Left: view from Siyeh Pass, looking down the valley of Rose Creek toward Saint Mary Lake, Glacier National Park, Montana

This land is their land ...

... and has been for many thousands of years. The front ranges of the Canadian Rockies are perfect bighorn sheep habitat: there are plenty of grassy meadows for grazing, with cliffs nearby to run to when the wolves and coyotes come. You can see bighorn sheep right beside the highways in the national parks. You can see them *on* the highway, out on the pavement, where they stand patiently licking the salty surface as trucks bear down on them.

Why don't they get out of the way? To a sheep, a truck is not a wolf or a cougar. Human hardware is not on the program for bighorns.

Signs in bighorn habitat warn motorists to slow down. All the better to stop, park safely on the shoulder and observe; the sheep are as tolerant of onlookers as they are of their cars, and enjoying a flock from a few paces away is one of the great national park experiences. An even better one: seeing the animals in a place like the one pictured, far from the nearest traffic jam of sheep-watchers.

Mule deer and white-tailed deer

It's no wonder that people confuse these two species. The tail of the white-tailed deer is not white, it's brown—until the animal flips it up, exposing the flashy white underside. The tail of the mule deer is white, with a black tip, and it does not turn that tail up; rather, it often wags its tail like a dog! Illustrated here we have a mule-deer buck in its gray winter coat and a white-tailed doe in its brown summer coat.

More common than white-taileds, mule deer are tolerant of humans in the national parks (no hunting allowed) and can be seen right in the park townsites, where they spend their time browsing on the ornamental shrubs of residents. The animals sleep in backyards, and they travel along the sidewalks with the other tourists. The white-taileds are shyer, seen on the fringes of built-up areas but not within.

It is important to remember that these are wild animals, capable of injuring humans. When cornered or otherwise frightened, and especially when they have fawns, the does will strike out with their hoofs. The impact can break ribs. The bucks sometimes attack with their antlers during the fall rut. As the park rules state explicitly, don't get close, and never feed them.

Alpenglow
(following page)

What is alpenglow? Nothing more than colored sunlight on rock and snow. But it's also nothing less.

Alpenglow is not limited to the Alps of Europe. Here we see it on the peaks of Waterton-Glacier International Peace Park. The sun has been down for hours at Upper Waterton Lake, now dimming into early evening, but high peaks such as Mt. Boswell intercept the last light as it beams across the Rockies from a sunset many miles away behind the camera. Atmospheric dust absorbs the blue wavelengths as the sun approaches the horizon, leaving only the reds and the pinks, the colors of alpenglow.

Above: aspen grove, Waterton-Glacier International Peace Park

Ants! More ants!

Only two heads are showing, but back in the tree there could be several more nestlings. And every one of them is constantly hungry. It's enough to keep a pair of flickers busy all day long. Like the other woodpeckers in our area, flickers eat mostly ants—especially the big black carpenter ants that plod over the forest floor. What the parents eat, the youngsters eat, too. Partly processed.

Left: female flicker with nestlings (Colaptes auratus)

Blue and White

The spikes of blue are lupine, a pea-family plant found in moist meadows. The lupines are especially common on the western side of the Rockies. Like the locoweeds, which are also members of the pea family, some lupines are poisonous to grazing animals, which don't eat them. Growing with lupine in this photo is white spirea, a woodland shrub with large flat flowerheads. It resembles its garden relatives.

Rime on the sedges ...

... announces overnight frost in a marsh near Whiteswan Lake. The frost has not struck hard; the creek is not frozen and the larch trees are still golden. The brown, iced-up sedges (those grass-like plants in the foreground) show that autumn is well on, and the wintry-looking peaks of the Hughes Range show that all will soon be snow-covered.

Above: **lupine** *(Lupinus sericeus),*
white spirea *(Spiraea betulifolia)*

Right: **Whiteswan Lake Provincial Park,**
British Columbia

These boulders may have come from that peak

Or they may not have, but chances are good that the rocks breaking up Mt. Aosta's reflection in Lower Elk Lake came from Mt. Aosta itself. Scooped out of Aosta's gray limestone is a glacial cirque that once functioned as a busy natural quarry. Fifteen thousand years ago that cirque was overflowing with ice; the glacier plucked away countless tons of Mt. Aosta and carried them into the valley now occupied by the lake. Nowadays only a small ice mass remains, hiding in the shadows of the cirque, but its handiwork still sticks up from the misty lake surface.

Big cat

Cougar, puma, mountain lion, panther—these are all names for the same cat. Here as everywhere, the cougar is a shy beast that lives very, very quietly. Your chances of seeing it are slim. You may see its tracks in the snow, though; they are about the size of those of a lynx or a bobcat, but they show a longer stride.

Cougars prefer low-elevation forests. They are more common on the western slope of the Canadian Rockies than on the eastern slope. Their favorite prey are deer, which they kill by biting either the throat (clamping down on the windpipe) or the top of the neck (breaking it by pulling it back or actually severing the bones). The cat has the wherewithal to do these things: very strong jaws and great big teeth. Is it dangerous to humans? On occasion, yes; there are several documented accounts in North America of young children having been killed by starving cougars. But we are far more dangerous to it, as we are to anything we consider a threat.

Left: Mt. Aosta (9823'/2994 m), in Elk Lakes Provincial Park, British Columbia

Above: cougar (Felis concolor)

*Left: spruce grouse
(Dendragapus
canadensis)*

Mountain chicken

Indeed, grouse are part of the same family of birds as turkeys and chickens. The red line above the eye and the black breast show that this spruce grouse is a male. The female is browner.

Spruce grouse are indeed dependent on spruce trees; they are one of the few creatures that eat conifer needles.

The second least-wary bird in the mountains (the least-wary is the ptarmigan, pages 48 and 92), the spruce grouse lets you approach within a few steps of it. Then, as you walk forward, it walks away. Charge toward a spruce grouse and it flaps awkwardly into the lower branches of a tree, where it sits at eye level, assuming that it's safe.

Headwaters

Mountains gather snow, and valleys gather the water melted from it. Splashing over Petain Falls is water melted from the Petain Glacier. That water is on its way to the Elk Lakes, the Elk River, the Kootenay and the Columbia rivers, and thus to the Pacific Ocean.

Right: Elk Lakes Provincial Park, British Columbia

The pattern of autumn

Poplars along the shore of Upper Kananaskis Lake flare into gold as the lower-growing vegetation goes crimson and burnt orange. Sky, mountains, trees and lakeshore—from top to bottom, this photo gives the pattern of autumn in the front ranges: blue, gray, green, gold and red.

Above: Upper Kananaskis Lake, Peter Lougheed Provincial Park, Alberta. From left to right: Mt. Fox (9754'/2973 m), two unnamed peaks, Mt. Foch (10433'/3180 m) and Mt. Sarrail (10413'/3174 m)

If you go out in the woods today ...

... you're in for a big surprise. Well, probably not; bears are shy animals, and you are unlikely to see one.

Bears in the Canadian Rockies come in two species: the American black bear and the grizzly bear *(see pages 8 and 96)*, which should really be called "brown bear" because it is the same species as the brown bear of Europe.

Black bears are forest bears; they stay below timberline most of the time. In contrast, Rockies grizzly bears are open-country creatures that prefer alpine meadows. This is why grizzly bears have a reputation for fierceness: on the tundra, there are no trees up which a female grizzly can send her cubs. She must stand and fight for them, which she is inclined to do.

If you are attacked by a grizzly—this is about as likely in the Canadian Rockies as getting hit by lightning—you should play dead. The bear will almost always assume that you are no longer a threat and withdraw. If attacked by a black bear, though, fight back: black bears seldom take on humans, but when they do they are predatory. In this case, playing dead is a bad idea; you are inviting the bear to eat you. Fortunately, black bears are rather easily driven off by yelling at them and hitting them with anything close at hand.

The usual problem people have with bears in the Rockies is much less serious: the bear is after the bacon. If your food is not locked in the trunk or well up a tree (and sometimes even if it is), the bear is going to get it. Don't ever feed a bear; this is the beginning of a sad sequence that usually results in the death of the bear.

Both species of mountain bears have to get as fat as possible in summer to survive a winter hibernation that can last seven months. Thus, when you see a bear it will probably be either eating or sleeping. It will not be primarily interested in you. It would prefer that you go away. You should.

Above right: black bear
(Ursus americanus)

33

Glacier lily

Like the shooting star, the glacier lily bends its petals backward, the better to expose the business part of the flower to the insects that pollinate it. Glacier lilies bloom early in the summer, springing up at the edges of melting snowbanks. Common in the Waterton-Glacier area, these elegant lilies are scarce north of central Banff National Park.

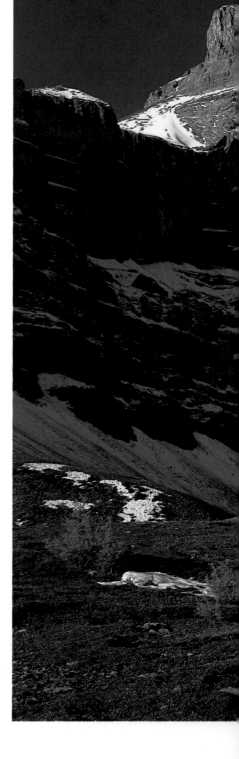

Above: glacier lily (Erythronium grandiflorum)

The Fortress

And a fitting name it is. The dark north face of the Fortress (9850'/3000 m) looks down half a mile (750 m) into the sunny valley below. Snow on ledges partway up highlights a prominent fold in the rock.

Like other front-range peaks in Kananaskis Country, the Fortress is made of seabed rock raised high above the waves some 85 million years ago. The summit block is of massive limestone, stronger than the shaly beds under it. Thus it has resisted erosion better and stands high above the boulder-dotted tundra.

Above: view from Fortress Ridge, Kananaskis Country, Alberta

High fall in the front ranges

Leaves of the poplar tribe are brightly pigmented with yellow carotene, but the color doesn't show through summer's deep-green chlorophyll. Photosynthesis ends with autumn frosts, though, and the green fades, allowing the yellow to come into its own. The slightest breeze sets the whole spectacle aflutter and gives this tree its name: "quaking aspen."

Alberta's provincial wildflower

At its showiest in late June, wild roses decorate moist meadows at lower elevations everywhere. They are true roses, with the characteristic rose fragrance, but the flowers open wider than the garden varieties. The color ranges from pale pink to brick red; occasionally you may see white ones.

Left: near the Kananaskis River in Kananaskis Country, Alberta. Mt. Kidd (9705'/2958 m) at left

Above: wild rose (Rosa acicularis)

Above: Smuts Creek, Mount Commonwealth and Mount Birdwood, Peter Lougheed Provincial Park, Alberta

Above: moose cow and calf (Alces alces)

In winter...

... moose eat mostly the ends of bushes for a living— "moose" means "twig-eater" in the Algonquin Indian language—but discovering an untouched patch of grass under the snow is good cause for this pair to get down on their knees. The larger one is the mother of the smaller one. Born in May, the calf has stayed with the cow through summer and fall, and it will remain with her until spring, when she chases it away just before delivering her next baby. *(see also page 87)*

Powdered by the clouds

Give a mountain a cloud and it will give the mountain some snow. The summit pyramid of Mt. Assiniboine reaches high into a misty October sky, where the peak's rock and ice surfaces have collected excess moisture unloaded in an overnight storm. The fog is burning off, leaving the mountains freshly powdered by the clouds.

The cold reaches down

Glaciers chill the flanks of Mt. Assiniboine, at 11,847' (3618 m) the highest peak in the southern Canadian Rockies. At the summit it is always winter. Here in the subalpine meadows along Magog Creek, the season of ice and snow is never far away, whether in distance or in time. Only ten weeks have gone by since the ground thawed in early July, and already the cold has reached down from the heights again.

Above: Mt. Magog (10,154'/3095 m) at left and Mt. Assiniboine (11,847'/3618 m) from Lake Magog , Mount Assiniboine Provincial Park, British Columbia

Right: Mount Assiniboine Provincial Park, British Columbia

The Rockwall at dawn

Golden-needled larch trees decorate subalpine meadows below the Rockwall: a line of peaks that forms an unbroken cliff 33 miles long (53 km). Here at Floe Lake, visible in the center of the photo, the Rockwall is 3000 feet high (900 m). Snow sliding down this remarkable cliff feeds glaciers along its base. Floe Lake lies against the ice, a fact made plain by the numbing cold of the water—and by the icebergs (the "floes") floating in it.

Left: view southwest from near Numa Pass, Kootenay National Park, British Columbia

Implications of a sawtooth horizon

At Floe Lake, dawn has to wait until the sun reaches over the surrounding peaks. Depending on its location, a particular patch of the mountain landscape can see a great deal of daylight or very little. Assuming a clear day, the top of a peak gets the most sunshine, receiving the morning rays hours before they reach the valley floors and enjoying extra late-afternoon warmth as well.

On the other hand, a deep gully in a north-facing cliff never sees direct sunlight. That is because, at the northerly latitude of the Canadian Rockies, the sun tracks no higher than 65 degrees above the southern horizon. Steep north-facing cliffs like the ones we see here are in shadow most of the year, which makes them perennially cold.

Amazingly, there are plants and animals that need just such an environment to survive. For example, a species aptly named the "ice insect" cannot tolerate warm temperatures. Held in a human hand, it dies.

In mountain ecology, each species of plant or animal has its own place in the sun—or not in the sun, as the case may be.

Canyon, Canadian-style

In the Canadian Rockies there are no big, winding, V-shaped, Grand-Canyon-style canyons. At one time there might have been, before the ice ages. But glaciers have since turned any sinuous V-shaped canyons into broad, straight, U-shaped ones. To Canadians, the limestone gorge in the picture is a canyon.

The origin of such gorges is problematic—some of them may have begun as caves—but they now represent the renewal of the erosion cycle, as the stream flowing through each begins to cut down into the valley floor. Give that baby canyon ten million years in which to grow, and perhaps it will become something like the Grand Canyon.

Above: Floe Lake, Kootenay National Park, British Columbia. View is southward along the Rockwall

Right: Marble Canyon, Kootenay National Park, British Columbia

Opabin Plateau ...

... is not a flat-topped mountain, so it is not really a plateau at all. Rather, Opabin Plateau is a flat-floored valley at timberline above Lake O'Hara. Canada has few proper plateaus (intense glaciation has seen to that), and it's no wonder that Canadians use the term oddly, just as they do the word "canyon" *(see page 44).*

However misnamed, Opabin Plateau is a mountain marvel. Rolling meadows are set about with scattered stands of Lyall's larch and subalpine fir; there are lots of boulder-edged reflecting ponds, and the great turreted peak of Mt. Huber (11,050′/3368 m) overlooks the lot.

The least of all chipmunks

To a wildlife biologist, "least" means "smallest." Thus, we have the "least sandpiper," the "least flycatcher," the "least weasel"—and the "least chipmunk," as if we were somehow dealing with a *quantity* of chipmunk.

In the Canadian Rockies this particular quantity of chipmunk hibernates for six months of the year—a long time to live on your body fat when you weigh only 45g (an ounce and a half)—and it puts on that fat by eating nothing but seeds. Presented with a ripe raspberry, for example, the least chipmunk eats only the tiny, hard kernels, leaving the sugary, calorie-laden fruit pulp for some other creature to enjoy.

This little rodent has an effective but mysterious defense against predators. Chipmunks are ground-dwelling and they venture far from their burrows; when a dog (and by extension, a coyote or a wolf) goes after one, it usually runs under a bush, squeaking loudly. In most instances the dog could easily catch the chipmunk, but it backs off. Why? The dog cannot tell us, but something has repelled it. Perhaps its ears are ringing from a sonic punch thrown at a pitch too high for humans to detect.

Left: Opabin Plateau is located above Lake O'Hara in Yoho National Park, British Columbia

Above: least chipmunk (Eutamias minimus)

Seasonal camouflage

Colors in the alpine zone change drastically with the seasons, and so does the plumage of the white-tailed ptarmigan. In summer the bird is virtually impossible to see at a distance its mottled coloration makes it look like any other rock on the tundra. In winter it becomes one with the snow.*(see page 92)*

So good is its camouflage, and so few are its enemies, that the ptarmigan is the least-wary bird in the mountains. People visiting the high country in early August are delighted when a ptarmigan hen and her chicks come clucking and peeping by, often walking right through a group of hikers. Cross-country skiers are sometimes surprised to see a dozen white heads pop up out of the snow around them, where the birds have sheltered overnight by burrowing in.

Above: **white-tailed ptarmigan** *(Lagopus leucurus)* ***in summer***

The conifer that isn't an evergreen

Strangest trees in the Canadian Rockies, the larches all practice the same unusual habit: they shed their needles in October. Before the needles go, they turn yellow-orange, putting on quite a show at timberline.

The species shown here is Lyall's larch *(Larix lyallii)*, named for naturalist and Rockies explorer David Lyall. Reaching thirty feet in height (9 m), Lyall's larch ignores the low-growing habit of its fellow timberline dwellers, the subalpine fir and the Engelmann spruce. The larch can afford to stand tall; it has no needles to hide from the fierce winter gales that freeze-dry the foliage of normal evergreens at such elevations.

Above: Lake McArthur, with Mt. Biddle (10,889'/3319 m) in the background, Yoho National Park, British Columbia

Left: gray jay
(Perisoreus canadensis)

Whiskey Jack

A folk name for the gray jay is "whiskey jack," adapted from the Cree "wis-kat-jon." People confuse the gray with its look alike cousin, Clark's nutcracker.*(see page 90)* Both have similar food-bumming habits, but the gray jay speaks more softly than Clark's nutcracker. Gray jays stay in the Canadian Rockies through the winter, while most of the nutcrackers leave, apparently preferring warmer climes to the west, in central British Columbia.

Along the Iceline

Perhaps the Yoho Valley's best, the Iceline Trail leads from one glacier to the next. This is exciting country; flowery alpine meadows run up against raw moraines of the Little Ice Age. In the photo we see paintbrush, both the red and yellow species; arnica (the other yellow flower), and many other bright spots against the green tundra. In the background, beyond the bouldery moraine, lies the blue-gray mass of Glacier des Poilus (pronounced "day-Poy-LOO," honoring a French general of World War I) encircling the base of Isolated Peak (9334'/2845 m).

Right:
Yoho National Park,
British Columbia

A rainless rainbow ...

... rides the mist above Twin Falls, in the Yoho Valley. The valley is famous for its waterfalls, but the photographer in this instance has chosen to secure something rarer: an ephemeral product of the water and the sun rather than the usual image of the falls themselves. Subalpine firs cling to the near skyline, and farther away the horn peak of Mt. Niles (9751'/2972 m) overlooks what remains of last winter's snow.

Lorquin's admiral

Butterflies have wonderful names. This one flits through the ponderosa-pine forests of the southern Rocky Mountain Trench, having metamorphosed from a caterpillar that fed on the leaves of willows, aspens, poplars and choke-cherry bushes. If it sees you, prepare to be buzzed: Lorquin's admiral is quite territorial. It chases other butterflies, and even small birds.

Left: Yoho National Park, British Columbia

Above: Lorquin's admiral (Limenitis lorquini)

The owl with the tail of a hawk

Most owls have short tails, but the northern hawk-owl has a long one. It's hawk-like in another way as well: it's active in the daytime, when most owls are sleeping. Nor does it hoot like other owls. It makes a squeaky sound, like glass being cleaned. Rather than perching partway up a tree and close to the trunk, where it can't be seen easily, the hawk-owl often chooses the top of a dead tree, such as the one pictured, from which to pounce on mice and other small rodents.

A bird of the far northern Rockies, the hawk-owl is rare south of Banff. Look for it at middle elevations, in heavy forest and wooded swampland.

Mummery Glacier

Like most Rockies glaciers, this one is only a remnant of its former self, but it's impressive nonetheless. Twenty thousand years ago the Mummery Glacier covered everything seen here.

The Canadian Rockies look the way they do—steep and rugged—because glaciers such as this one have been whittling away at the mountains for at least two million years and probably for a lot longer than that. Glaciers straighten winding stream courses; they cut the valleys wider and thus leave the valley walls steeper. They grind away rock much more quickly than running water does, which is why an ice age is such an effective landscape modifier. All the high mountain ranges on earth are currently glaciated—even equatorial ranges such as the central Andes.

Glaciers and mountains go together; without the mountain uplands to collect the snow, there would be no glaciers south of the Arctic Circle. Without the glaciers, there would be no reservoirs of ice to keep the mountain rivers flowing full all summer long, months after the snow at lower elevations has melted. Look at the amount of water being given up by that veteran ice front in the photograph. Downstream, a million living things need every drop.

Human beings are warming the world's climate far faster than nature did at the end of the last ice age 11,000 years ago. Some scientists think we may lose about half the glacial ice in the Rockies over the next fifty years. Over a hundred years we may lose it all. What then?

Above: northern hawk-owl (Surnia ulula)

Right: above the Blaeberry River, British Columbia

Above: beaver (Castor canadensis)

Enjoy this cliché while it lasts

No pictorial treatment of the Canadian Rockies would be complete without a shot of Mt. Rundle reflected in the Vermilion Lakes. This scene is a classic.

Not many viewers realize, though, how ephemeral it is. The Vermilion Lakes are essentially beaver ponds. Recently one of the main beaver dams was breached by agents unknown—most likely it was the beavers themselves, which have been known to do that when they are ready to move on—and the water level dropped considerably, turning much of this particular reflecting pool into a non-reflecting mud flat.

Above: view southeastward toward Tunnel Mountain (5546'/1690 m) at left and Mt. Rundle (9675'/2949 m) at center, near Banff, Alberta

A-honk, a-honk

It may mean "back off!" Or it may mean "I love you." Whether courting their mates or threatening a nearby pair that is getting too close, Canada geese are lots of fun to watch. They're not particularly shy, either; often you can get close—especially on the mountain-resort golf courses this bird seems to prefer. That stands to reason; Canada geese eat mostly grass, and the greens are pretty tasty. Of course, the weed-killers dumped on those greens are not good for the birds. They do best in their natural habitat—shallow ponds in marshy places.

Most other species of waterfowl are on the decline in North America, due to an ongoing drought on the prairies that has dried up the ponds and marshes the birds need for migration and raising their young. Intentional draining by farmers has aggravated the problem. But the Canada goose is not as dependent on water as its relatives, and its numbers have increased accordingly.

Above: **Canada geese** *(Branta canadensis)*

Glad not to be a fish

The young osprey on the nest looks startled. Perhaps it is considering how deadly those approaching talons are. If that were a parent bird approaching, the juveniles on the nest would have nothing to fear, but in this case it's another juvenile trying to steal a fish from its nestmates. (Yes; the youngster flying in *did* steal the fish.)

A pair of ospreys will build an enormous nest in the top of a broken-off conifer—or on any lofty perch overlooking the water, such as a power-line pole—and will return to it every spring. In our part of the world they winter on the West Coast. Like other bird species in which the male and female are colored similarly, the osprey mates for life, or, as is so often the case in the natural world, for the few seasons that pass before its mate is no more.

Above: osprey (Pandion haliaetus)

Call it what you will

The nomenclature applied to this animal is haywire. Elk should really be called either "wapiti," which means "white rear end" in Shawnee (the official Canadian name, which fits them perfectly), or "red deer," which is the name of the species in Britain. "Elk" in Europe refers to a different animal entirely: the moose. Further, the sexes are correctly "stags" and "hinds," as per the original British usage, rather than "bulls" and "cows," as one hears on this side of the Atlantic. *(see also page 104)*

The front ranges

Note that "front ranges" is not capitalized. It's generic, and it refers to one of the three great divisions of the Canadian Rockies. The other two are the main ranges to the west and the foothills to the east.

The Rockies were built in stages. The main ranges came first, rising above sea level about 120 million years ago. The rock in them is old, up to 730 million years. As the disturbance spread eastward, the front ranges began to rise some 85 million years ago; they are made of rock that is somewhat younger than that of the main ranges. The foothills were last, beginning to grow about 65 million years ago, and they have the youngest rock. Thus the Rockies have a remarkable geological symmetry: the oldest part (the main ranges) has the oldest rock; the middle-aged part (the front ranges) has middle-aged rock, and the youngest part (the foothills) has the youngest rock.

This autumn photograph of the Sawback Range, a typical front-range ridge running northwest from Banff, shows two other characteristics of the front ranges: the rock is mostly limestone and shale, and it is steeply tilted.

Above: wapiti or bull elk (Cervus elaphus)

Right: view northeast from the Bow Valley Parkway in central Banff National Park, Alberta

Red-and-yellow columbine

A red species of columbine grows on the western slope of the Canadian Rockies, and a yellow species grows on the eastern slope. Near the continental divide the two species sometimes interbreed, producing unusual red-and-yellow flowers such as this one.

Has-been Matterhorn

Pilot Mountain is a horn peak: a summit sharpened by glaciers gnawing from all sides. So is the Matterhorn of Switzerland, and so is the Rockies' own Mt. Assiniboine. But Pilot Mountain has been over-glaciated, chewed down to 9630 feet (2945 m) from loftier heights in times past. The peak is now too low to support glaciers; the whitening near the summit is only snow.

Struggling under the Castle

The elk in this photo have several tough months ahead of them. An elk cannot get enough nourishment from under the snow to meet all its needs. Thus, it enters the fall as plump as it can get and loses weight all winter under the strain of an ongoing food deficit. In effect, it starves as slowly as possible.

Normally its body fat will see it through, but the animal has a backup nutrient supply for use at the end of an especially long or difficult winter: its bone marrow. The marrow of ungulates is quite fatty, as eaters of steak may have noticed. When all other reserves are gone, an elk can scrape by for a couple of weeks on its marrow. Those couple of weeks often come in April, after last-year's grass has lost most of its nutritive value to under-snow rot, and this-year's grass has not yet appeared.

When T.S. Eliot wrote that "April is the cruellest month," he might have been speaking about the creatures you see in this picture. Wish them luck. They're going to need it.

Right: coyote
(Canis latrans)

Live smart

There are three species of the dog family in the Canadian Rockies: foxes, wolves and coyotes. Of these, coyotes are the most numerous and most visible. Any picnic ground in the national parks will have a coyote on the fringes, waiting patiently for the picnickers to leave. Some coyotes are so bold that they stand a few steps away from the table, looking like the family dog. This encourages the giving of handouts, which is bad for both parties: when the tidbits are gone, the coyote can get nasty and the hander-outer can get bitten. In turn, the wardens kill the coyote. Don't feed wild animals.

A pack of coyotes will go yipping and yapping through a park campground in the wee hours, scaring the campers. Probably they're looking for goodies, but maybe they do it for fun as well. Some biologists swear that coyotes have a sense of humor. Otherwise why would they steal golf balls from the greens at mountain resorts?

Coyotes do just fine without humans, of course. In the summer they bounce around in meadows, catching mice and ground squirrels. In the winter they follow wolf packs, slinking over to clean up a kill when the wolves have eaten all they can hold.

Above left: herd of female
elk in a meadow under
Castle Mountain, central
Banff National Park

Flowers hiding among bracts

Common at all elevations, paintbrush comes in shades of red, pink and purple. Occasionally you'll see white-tipped pink paintbrush. A couple of species are yellow; one of them, alpine yellow paintbrush, is a tundra wildflower.

Paintbrush is known and loved across western North America, but few of its admirers are aware that the colorful parts of the plant are not flowers. They are bracts, which are modified leaves. The flowers are the green spikes poking out among the bracts. Another little-known fact about paintbrush: the plant is a parasite. Its roots attach to those of other plants, from which it steals nourishment. (Paintbrush also produces some of its own food, through its own small leaves.)

Paintbrush and pearly everlasting ...

... decorate a hillside with the colors of Canada's flag: red and white. That's oddly appropriate; the mountains across the way, rising above morning mist in the valley of Moraine Lake, are part of the Ten Peaks chain, arguably the nation's favorites. Left to right: Bident Mountain (10,118'), four-summited Mt. Quadra (10,410'), rocky Mt. Babel (10,174'), Mt. Little (10,302'), Mt. Bowlen (10,079') and, in the sun at right, Mt. Allen (10,860').

Above: paintbrush (Castilleja species)

Right: south of Lake Louise in Banff National Park, Alberta

*Above: **pika** (Ochotona princeps)*

Rock rabbit

Coloradoans call them "coneys"; Canadians call them "pikas" (rhymes with how New Yorkers say "hikers"). Pikas are, indeed, members of the same order as rabbits and hares—all are lagomorphs—but pikas are in their own family. Odd little animals, they scurry about among the boulders that lie in great heaps at the bases of cliffs. Pikas gather vegetation in the late summer and dry it on flat rocks in the fall. Then they carry it below and line their boulder-runs with it. Non-hibernators, what they do down there all winter long is anyone's guess—although they must spend some of their time creating more pikas, because the little ones are born in May.

Incidentally, we should all really be saying "peek-a," not "pie-ka." The word is Siberian, and it imitates the sound a pika makes.

Canada's twenty-dollar view

Sunrise touches the greatest mountain wall in the Canadian Rockies. Stretching for six miles (10 km) and standing 3500 feet (1000 m) above Moraine Lake, the Wenkchemna Peaks are familiar to every Canadian: they appear on the country's twenty-dollar bill. "Wenkchemna" means "ten" in the language of the Stoney Indians—thus the name "Valley of the Ten Peaks" for this area—but the Stoneys never knew the range by that designation. A Philadelphia mountaineer named Samuel Allen gave it that name in the 1890s.

Allen was a student of linguistics at Yale University. He was much taken with native North American languages, and he numbered the peaks from one to ten in Stoney on a detailed map of the area he published in 1896. The Indians were not consulted; their names for the Ten Peaks, if they had any, are unknown. Most of the Ten Peaks have since been renamed for people, but Peak Four ("Tonsa"), Peak Nine ("Neptuak") and Peak Ten ("Wenkchemna") retain Allen's appellations.

Above from left to right: Mt. Bowlen (Peak Three, "Yamnee," 10,079'/3072 m), Peak Four ("Tonsa," 10,020'/3054 m), Mt. Perren (Peak Five, "Sapta," 10,860'/3051 m), Mt. Allen (Peak Six, originally "Shappee," renamed for Samuel Allen, 10,860'/3310 m), Mt. Tuzo (Peak Seven, "Sagowa," 10,646'/3245 m), Mt. Deltaform (Peak Eight, "Saknowa," at 11,234'/3424 m the highest of the Ten Peaks) and Neptuak Mountain (Peak Nine, "Neptuak," 10,620'/3237 m).
Banff National Park, Alberta

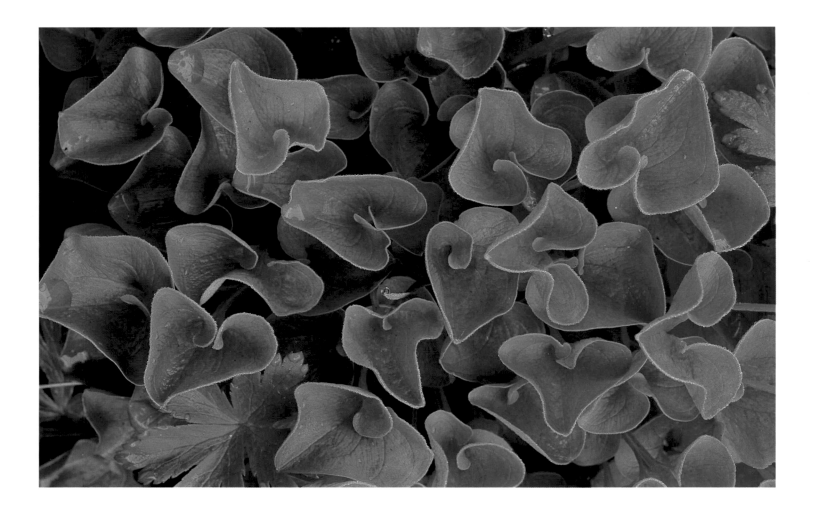

Ice into water

A vertical mile above Paradise Creek, the summit of Mt. Temple collects snow all winter—a lot of snow, enough to produce that lovely white glacier in the picture. The summer sun hits the winter accumulation and melts some of it, but not all of it, or the glacier would not be there. On a hot July day enough snowmelt runs down Mt. Temple—and enough snow slides down as avalanches, then melts at the bottom—to fill Paradise Creek from bank to bank.

If you were to view Paradise Creek late at night, you would find less than half the amount of water you saw at three o'clock in the afternoon. Like other meltwater streams, Paradise Creek roars through the heat of the day but gurgles quietly in the wee hours.

Here's the kicker. Paradise Creek can be crossed at almost any point early in the morning, when climbers are on their approach to Mt. Temple, but in the afternoon the stepping stones are well under the waves. What do the climbers do? They look for another crossing point, and if there isn't one they sit and wait. It can be a long wait.

Left: Mt. Temple (11,624'/3543 m) was first climbed by Samuel Allen, Louis Frissel and Walter Wilcox in 1894. View is from the Paradise Valley Trail, south of Lake Louise in Banff National Park, Alberta

Moisture-catchers

Anyone with a macro lens in his camera bag would have trouble passing up a shot like this. Later in the summer this plant colony will bloom, and the flowers are also photogenic: five white, very frilly petals. The name? Fringed grass-of-parnassus. It's most common at timberline, growing along creeks, and it blooms in late July.

Above: fringed grass-of-parnassus (Parnassia fimbriata)

Above: view west across Lake Louise toward the
Upper Victoria Glacier, Banff National Park, Alberta

Lake glow

Lake Louise seems to glow bluish green in this unusual view of one of the more famous scenes in the Canadian Rockies. Behind the photographer was an eight-story hotel full of tourists, but few would have been up and about at dawn, which comes at 5:30 a.m. in midsummer, when the picture was taken.

The lake color comes from rock flour (fine glacial scrapings) suspended in the water. These microscopic particles tend to scatter the light, giving the lake its milky look.

What we see reflected in the lake is morning alpenglow. Morning alpenglow is like the more familiar evening alpenglow, but with a subtle difference: the atmosphere is not as dusty in the morning, because dust stirred up by daytime creatures (such as humans) has settled overnight, and thus morning alpenglow is not as red.

Contrast this gentle scene with its forbiddingly beautiful winter aspect.

Above: winter scene, Lake Louise, Banff National Park, Alberta

High-country woodchuck

Woodchucks (biologists prefer "woodchuck" to "groundhog") don't live in the Canadian Rockies, although they range closely to the east and west. Instead of the woodchuck, we have an alpine representative of the clan: the hoary marmot. It has an enviable lifestyle: it awakens in May, spends the summer stuffing itself full of tundra vegetation, mates, then goes back to bed in September.

A folk name for the marmot is "whistler," which is why there is a mountain called The Whistlers above the town of Jasper, and a place called Whistler in British Columbia. Both commemorate the loud, one-note call of this big, easygoing rodent.

No one had to plant this garden

And no human looks after it, although a myriad of small vegetarians—field mice, marmots, snowshoe hares, pikas—eat what it grows. Birds, bears and grazing animals spread the seeds. Summer lasts only two months here, so everything blooms at once: scarlet paintbrush and yellow arnica, purple fleabane and the strange green spheres of longstem greencaps. Hidden in the lush foliage are dozens more species. Compare this delicate scene with a winter view of a similar place, as shown on page 112.

Above: **hoary marmot** (Marmota caligata)

Right: **along the trail to Hidden Lake, east of Lake Louise in Banff National Park, Alberta**

Marmot?

Nope. But lots of people think it is. This is the Columbian ground squirrel. It lives in meadows at all elevations in the Canadian Rockies. Smaller than a marmot, it says "tweep!" when alarmed, rather than emitting a loud whistle as marmots do. Like other ground squirrels, this one hibernates. Colonies of Columbian ground squirrels provide good sport for grizzly bears, who like to dig 'em up and eat' em.

Right: Columbian ground squirrel
(Spermophilus columbianus)

Colossus in the alpine meadows

Redoubt Mountain, named for a type of fortification used in World War I (many peaks of the Canadian Rockies were named during and immediately after that war), rears above the flowery alpine meadows in and about Boulder Pass. Common species visible include arnica (bright yellow), alpine paintbrush (pale yellow) and daisy-like fleabane (purple). Ptarmigan Lake is visible under the peak.

Why are meadows like this one so extensive in the Canadian Rockies? It's because timberline is so low—7500 feet (2300 m) here, near Lake Louise—and some thirty percent of the land surface lies above that elevation.

On the day this picture was taken, the fragrance of wildflowers sweetened the air, while Columbian ground squirrels, pikas and marmots busily gathered the natural bounty around them.

Left: Banff National Park, Alberta

High water on Bow Lake
(following page)

The low-growing willows are inundated, and this species can't survive for long that way, which means that the water is unusually high. So much snowmelt is flowing in that the outlet stream can't keep up with it. In a few days, though, things will equalize.

Speaking of the outlet stream: it's the Bow River. Bow Lake is the headwaters of the Bow River, unless you consider the headwaters to be Bow Glacier, which feeds the lake. Passed from the Bow to the Saskatchewan and the Nelson, that water flooding the willows will eventually wind up in Hudson Bay.

Following page: left to right—Bow Peak (9409'/2868 m)
and Crowfoot Mountain (10,007'/3050 m),
in Banff National Park north of Lake Louise, Alberta

Bunny

There are no rabbits in the Canadian Rockies. Instead, we have hares—snowshoe hares. Mottled brown in summer, snowshoe hares go pure white in winter; thus their other name: varying hare. This bunny has big back feet, and its tracks are disproportionately large for its size. The set in the photo shows that the hare was travelling toward the camera; in hopping, the species places its back feet ahead of its front feet.

Atmosphere ...

... is what the romantic painters called it: the peaks fading with distance, each row fainter than the one before. Atmosphere in the Rockies comes from the smoke of forest fires, most of which are not natural. Logged lands to the west are intentionally burned by the loggers, to get rid of the unwanted branches of cut trees. The practice also makes replanting easier.

The "slash-burning" season begins in August and runs well into the fall. If you want photographs that feature the crystal air for which the Canadian Rockies are famous, you had better get there before the loggers light up. Or hope for easterly winds.

Left: tracks of a snowshoe hare (Lepus americanus)
View north from near Bow Summit,
off the Icefields Parkway in central
Banff National Park, looking down the valley of the
Mistaya River ("Mistaya" is the Stoney Indian word
for grizzly bear). Peyto Lake lies frozen below

Above: view north from Bow Pass,
Banff National Park, Alberta

The main ranges

The Canadian Rockies do not readily subdivide into geographically isolated groups, as do the Rockies of Wyoming, Colorado or New Mexico. Thus, the use of geographical range names in the Canadian Rockies has proved impractical, even though maps make the attempt. Geologically, though, the whole area breaks down into three parts, and these three geological subdivisions—from east to west, the foothills, front ranges and main ranges—are more often applied than the geographical ones.

The peak in the picture is typical of the main ranges: the backbone of the Rockies, the continental divide. Here the rock is old. It dates back to the early and middle parts of the Cambrian geological period, ranging from 570 million years at the base to 530 million years at the top. Originally laid down as sediment in the sea, this rock was thrust into mountains beginning about 120 million years ago. So much erosion has occurred during and after mountain-building (five or six vertical miles of rock removed—eight to ten kilometres) that the modern landscape bears little resemblance to the Rockies of ages past. The last two million years, especially, have seen great changes as ice-age glaciers carved the peaks steeper and gouged the valleys deeper, wider and straighter.

The geological message of this incredible landscape, as complex as it seems, is surprisingly simple: old rock, deposited grain by grain in the sea; middle-aged mountains, formed about the same time as the Alps, and a young landscape, freshly glaciated.

Fierce exterior, heart of gold

Think of the porcupine as a large arboreal rodent, which is what it is. Mainly active at night, porcupines eat aspen and poplar leaves when they can, bark and conifer needles when they can't. They don't hibernate. They have a fondness for the soft green needles of Lyall's larch, found near timberline from Lake Louise south. They like to be alone, mostly, although sometimes two of them will share a tree—especially during mating season.

That brings up a prickly question: how do porcupines do it? Answer: very carefully. This is the oldest joke in biology.

You still want to know? She flips up her tail, which has no spines underneath. This provides a protective pad for him; he mounts her in standard mammal fashion.

Stories abound of porcupines chewing things: outhouse seats, wooden handles, brake lines on automobiles. Recent research has shown that porkies do this because they crave sodium. Salt is the best source of sodium, so the porkies seek it out. They find it in dried sweat and urine, and they find it under automobiles that have travelled Canada's heavily salted highways. Many kinds of paint are rich in sodium too, which explains the critter's predilection for gnawing signs in the woods.

The porcupine is harmless to us, as long as we don't touch it. It can't throw its quills, as some people think; when cornered, it turns its back to the enemy, protecting its vulnerable face, and switches its tail from side to side. The quills detach very easily. Many a dog has learned that the hard way.

Above: porcupine (Erethizon dorsatum)

Braided river

Wide and shallow, the North Saskatchewan River carries silt, sand and gravel dumped into it from glaciers upstream. The water is moving too slowly here to transport the whole load, so it deposits the excess in the form of gravel bars. As the bars grow, the water runs among them in multiple channels that shift by the hour, joining here and splitting there. From the air, the flood plain looks braided—a distinctive feature of glacial rivers like this one.

Second-largest land animal in North America

The largest? The bison.

Bull moose are usually solitary, although several of them sometimes stick together in winter (behavior known as "yarding up") to share good survival spots and to defend more effectively against their main predators, packs of wolves. The bull in the photo, raising its head to peer at the photographer from the swamp in which it is eating water plants, has a good start on growing the current year's set of antlers.

Above: seen in evening light, peaks in the background are, from left to right, Mt. Chephren (10,715'/3266 m), White Pyramid (10,745'/3275 m), Epaulette Mountain (10,154'/3095 m), the Kaufmann Peaks (left 10,203'/3110 m, right 10,154'/3095 m), named for two famous mountain guides, Hans and Christian Kaufmann, who were brothers from Switzerland, and Mt. Sarbach (10,351'/3155 m), named for Peter Sarbach, another early Swiss guide.
Northern Banff National Park, Alberta

Right: bull moose (Alces alces)

Layers

Geologists have long delighted in the Canadian Rockies, for these mountains preserve one of the better geological records to be found anywhere in the world. Here the sedimentary stack is 20 miles thick (30 km), with few unrepresented gaps in time.

The oldest layers, found in the Waterton-Glacier area, hold clues to events 1.5 billion years ago; the youngest strata, found in the Rocky Mountain Trench on the western slope, were laid down just before the ice ages—quite recently, in geological terms. Deposits left by the glaciers themselves bring the record up to the present.

Of course, no particular mountain could possibly show the whole sequence. A single mountain is not big enough, nor could a 20-mile-high peak do the job if one existed. While one part of the Rockies was receiving sediment, another was not, so the record must be reconstructed from various sites. Further, mountain-building has broken up the pile, folding the layers and making a mess of things.

A hundred years of geological research, though, has sorted the Canadian Rockies out. Within the limestone and shale beds in the picture, geologists have found what they need—trilobites, brachiopods, graptolites—to determine the time of deposition and the living conditions during the period represented.

Here is a one-sentence summary of what they have learned: the whole area lay under the sea for most of its long history, until a collision of crustal plates crumpled the layers upward, forming the Rockies over a 75-million year period that began about 120 million years ago.

Most beautiful wildflower in the Rockies?

Lots of people think so. Besides, it's an orchid and thereby endowed with a special loveliness.

This is the calypso orchid, also called fairy-slipper or Venus's-slipper. It's not very tall—about six inches (15 cm)—but it often grows in groups, catching the eye with a burst of color a few steps off the trail. Look for it in wooded places between mid-May and mid-June.

Above left: Mt. Erasmus
(10,712'/3265 m) in northern
Banff National Park, Alberta

Above: calypso orchid (Calypso bulbosa)

A glimpse back into the Pleistocene ...

... is possible from this viewpoint on Parker Ridge. A walk of about an hour ends here, in sight of the Saskatchewan Glacier, headwaters of the North Saskatchewan River, and at its head, under the cloud, a view of the Columbia Icefield. Spectacular as it seems, the view is limited; most of the ice mass lies out of sight over the horizon. Here we see less than ten percent of the 125 square miles (325 km^2) that make the Columbia Icefield the largest glacier in the Rockies. It's a view right out of the ice ages.

The prominent dark line in the photo is a medial moraine, a stripe of boulders marking the place where a side glacier joined the main glacier from the right, out of sight around the corner. The peak in the background is Castleguard Mountain (10,138'/3090 m), which supports its own glacier.

Unseen in the rock below is Castleguard Cave, the longest known cavern in Canada (ten miles/16 km), whose main passage lies under the Columbia Icefield. The cave ends in glacial ice, where explorers reach something they can see nowhere else in the world: the belly of an icefield.

*Above: **northern Banff National Park, Alberta***

Rawk, rawk, rawk ...

... all day long. If you pull into the Columbia Icefield Campground, or any other well-used overnighting site near timberline in the Canadian Rockies, this is what you will hear. It comes from Clark's nutcracker, most insistent vocalist of the jay tribe. Young birds are especially noisy, following their long-suffering parents around, squawking constantly.

All the corvids (jays, ravens, crows, magpies, nutcrackers) are very intelligent birds; Clark's nutcracker is able to remember the location of at least 2000 hidden items of food. Some of those items may be lifted from your picnic table when you're looking the wrong way.

*Right: **Clark's nutcracker** (Nucifraga columbiana)*

Above: white-tailed ptarmigan (Lagopus leucurus) in winter

Moon in the Saddle

Indeed, the name of the landform cradling the moon is the "Saddle," a high, glacier-bearing pass on Mt. Athabasca (11,453′/3491 m). The horn of the Saddle, at left, is the oft-climbed "Silverhorn," one of Mt. Athabasca's two summits (the main summit is just out of view farther left).

The Saddle sees even more mountaineers than the Silverhorn. Climbing to the Saddle affords the easiest route to the top.

Above: telephoto view from near Wilcox Pass, southern Jasper National Park, Alberta

The glaciers are going

On the skyline we see the white rim of the Columbia Icefield. The dark cliffs below are 3000 feet high (900 m). At their base lies a dying glacier—the Dome Glacier, which has been retreating for about 150 years. Its former size is shown by the vacated glacial bed, bare and brown; a lateral moraine on the left side (the ridge-like feature at center left in the photo) gives some idea of the former thickness of the ice. Glaciers in the Canadian Rockies reached their greatest extent since the end of the ice ages in the mid-1840s, the Little Ice Age, when the climate was cooler than it is now.

There is more ice here than meets the eye. The stripe of white in the center is bare glacier, but filling the valley to the right and left of it is more of the same hidden under a covering of fallen rock.

Above: view from Mt. Wilcox westward toward the Snow Dome (11,352'/3460 m), in southern Jasper National Park, Alberta. Peak at right is Mt. Kitchener (11,519'/3511 m)

A gentle, violent animal

Wilderness icons that they are, bighorn sheep are still sheep: placid grazers most of the time. But these are not domesticated animals; the wildness has not been bred out of them. Among the rams, that wildness asserts itself daily, in the form of ongoing head-butting matches. Through the summer the horn-whacking is pretty casual—a tap here, a tap there—to keep the hierarchy straight. In November and December, though, at the height of the rut, the rams engage each other with real ferocity. They back off far enough to meet on the run, and the impact can send both combatants reeling away. Horn tips split and break off. A poorly parried blow can break the skull.

Fortunately for humans, bighorn rams don't see us as sexual adversaries. But it's still wise to stand well clear while watching an all-out contest.

*Above: **bighorn sheep** (Ovis canadensis)*

95

Above: **grizzly bear, Jasper National Park, Alberta**
(Also see page 8)

Color on the outwash flats

Red paintbrush *(Castilleja)* and pink river beauty *(Epilobium latifolium)* colonize gravel carried away from glaciers not far upstream. Life on these outwash flats is tenuous. One year the river might spare this patch of color from its spring flood; the next year it might wash it away, or bury it under new outwash. Only a week after the picture was taken, heavy rains carried the flowers off. Within a year or two, though, the river beauty will be back.

Right: **looking south up the Sunwapta River toward Mt. Athabasca (11453'/3491 m) and its northern (unnamed) glacier, Jasper National Park, Alberta**

Some of the water stops ...

... but most keeps flowing under the ice. Winter is long in the Canadian Rockies; streams and lakes begin to freeze in October and don't thaw until April (until June at higher elevations). Waterfalls freeze last, because they have the swiftest flow. On the other hand, the ice buildup on waterfalls is so thick that it lasts for weeks after the ice of lakes and streams has disappeared.

Edges and ledges

Imagine a stack of paper lying flat on a desk. Now bend up the edge of the pile that's facing away from you. Take an imaginary knife to that edge, trimming away some of the sheets, and sift powdered sugar over the whole thing. You have a reasonable facsimile of the scene in this photograph. Layers of Cambrian and Ordovician sediments have been bent upward away from the photographer; the layers in the trees are nearly flat-lying, producing snowy ledges, while those on the horizon are steeply tilted. Erosion has cut into the stack, exposing the edges of the layers.

Left: Tangle Falls, along the Icefields Parkway in southern Jasper National Park, Alberta

Above: looking west from the Icefields Parkway toward an unnamed peak in the Winston Churchill Range, southern Jasper National Park, Alberta

From the ashes, an unusual phoenix

A forest fire has given the ecological cycle another turn. Among the early colonizers of burned-over land is strawberry blite. A member of the goosefoot family, strawberry blite is not a strawberry at all (strawberries belong to the genus *Fragaria*), nor does "blite" refer to some sort of affliction (as in "blight"). It's simply an old name for the goosefoot family, of which strawberry blite is a well-known member.

*Above: **strawberry blite** (Chenopodium capitatum)*

Springboard for the sun's rays

Smoke from a distant forest fire has reddened the sky at dawn. The smoke gives the atmosphere substance; the great quartzite slabs of Endless Chain Ridge cast their shadows on the air itself, as sunlight from over the horizon streams through.

Above: Endless Chain Ridge runs for nine miles (15 km) along the eastern side of the Icefields Parkway in southern Jasper National Park, Alberta

From cement gray to milky blue
(following page)

All summer, the glacier-fed Athabasca River runs gray, loaded with particles of rock flour: microscopic flakes ground from the bedrock by moving glacial ice. In the fall, though, glacial melt slackens and so does the amount of rock flour delivered to the Athabasca River. The water clarifies, although it always carries a cloudy glacial tinge.

Following page: in the background, Mt. Fryatt 11,027' (3361 m) is covered with fall snow. Jasper National Park, Alberta

Wapiti

Elk stags are at their best in the fall. Strong from a summer of good eating, they enter the mating season—the rut—with their white-tipped antlers sharp and ready, and their bodies full of hormones that make them aggressive toward other stags. They also threaten any other creature that approaches them, such as a human with a camera. Keep your distance.

Hinds (cows) gather around the stag with the biggest antlers. This makes good genetic sense, for a fine rack is the mark of a successful animal, one with good genes to pass on to the next generation. Well-matched stags lock antlers, pushing and shoving as the hinds watch; he who has his head forced to the ground loses, and the winner takes all.

Sad to say, today's victor is tomorrow's wolf food. A constantly rutting stag eats very little during September and October, so he enters the cold months vulnerably low on fat reserves. The average life span of a stag in the Canadian Rockies is only a few years past maturity; that of a hind ten or fifteen. The counts tell the tale: three out of four adult animals in any particular herd are females.

First touch of autumn

The green is going, the gold coming on. Quaking aspen, a member of the poplar tribe, shares that yellow color with its relatives the cottonwoods. To differentiate aspens (Populus tremuloides) from cottonwoods or other poplars, look at the bark: it's white and smooth on aspen, gray and furrowed on the other species.

Left: bull elk (Cervus elaphus)

Above: in the background, Windy Castle (9252'/2820 m), seen east of the Icefields Parkway south of Athabasca Falls in Jasper National Park, Alberta

Plunge pool

In summer Sunwapta Falls is a spectacle, well-attended by admiring crowds. The Sunwapta River, full from bank to bank, pours over the cliff in the background and pounds through this gorge. But the winter flow of the Sunwapta is only five percent of its summer flow, which is the norm for glacially fed rivers in the Canadian Rockies, and a look into the gorge in January reveals a study in serenity. The waterfall has frozen solid, but that five-percent flow sneaks under it to the pool, disturbing the surface just enough to keep it from freezing.

The winter visitor has this scene all to himself.

Minus forty

Yes, it gets cold in the Canadian Rockies. Canadians reckon their frost in degrees Celsius, Americans in degrees Fahrenheit. Converting requires number-crunching, but -40° is the same temperature in either system: frigid.

At forty below, any open water, even water that is close to freezing, is considerably warmer than the atmosphere. Moisture evaporating from the surface becomes visible as it condenses in the frigid air producing vapor.

The view is of the Athabasca River near Athabasca Falls. In the background are two peaks with no official names. (Yes, there are still unnamed peaks in the Rockies.) Their local names are "Geraldine Peak" (9646'/2940 m, on the left) and "Whirlpool Peak" (9547'/2910 m, on the right).

Left: central Jasper National Park, Alberta

Above: looking west from the Icefields Parkway in Jasper National Park, Alberta

Dawn on the Ramparts

Banff National Park has its Ten Peaks; Jasper National Park has the Ramparts. This is another of the Rockies' great mountain walls, stretching for eight miles (13 km) along the continental divide. Here we see a short section of the Ramparts from Amethyst Lakes—a single lake, really, divided into northern and southern parts by a peninsula. The elevation at the lakes is 6450 feet (1960 m), just below timberline. The summit elevation of Dungeon Peak, in the center of the photo, is 10,269 feet (3130 m), for a total relief of over 3800 feet (1160 m).

The rocks in the foreground are lichen-covered quartzite blocks derived from the Ramparts themselves. Small glaciers nestle at the base of the wall, one of them tucked behind a textbook example of a terminal moraine. The larger ancestors of these modern glaciers spread those boulders. Not visible from any highway, this scene requires a trail trip of 11.6 miles (18.7 km). It's worth it.

Left: from left to right, Oubliette Mountain (10,138'/3090 m), Dungeon Peak (10,269'/3130 m), Redoubt Peak (10,236'/3120 m), all seen from the east. First ascended in the 1920s along the ridges and by their easier western sides (not seen here), the peaks of the Ramparts were not climbed directly up the cliffs until the 1960s and 1970s. Western Jasper National Park, Alberta

Tundra deer

Caribou are indeed members of the deer family, but they are deer adapted to life in the high country. The reindeer of Europe is the same animal.

In summer caribou eat mainly lichens (fungal-algal combinations that grow bountifully on the tundra from Saskatchewan Crossing north), supplemented with grasses, sedges and wildflowers. In winter, caribou paw through the deepening snow to reach their meals—"caribou" comes from an Algonquin word meaning "the one that scratches"—but eventually the snow becomes so deep that they must switch to lichens growing on trees, for which they move below timberline. Here the snow is deepest of all, and caribou have big feet for helping them move through it.

Caribou grow and shed antlers each year, as do their ungulate relatives the mule deer, elk and moose, but unlike these species, caribou of both sexes carry antlers, not just the males. The caribou pictured here are all bulls, and they are showing behavior typical of their species: standing around on a summer snowbank to escape the bugs.

Above: caribou (Rangifer tarandus)

109

The high country

Head uphill anywhere in the Canadian Rockies and you will encounter a scene like this one, in which most of what you see is above timberline. Forty percent of Jasper National Park, where this picture was taken, lies above the trees. Most park visitors stay on the valley floors, where the forest dominates; the alpine meadows seem far away, the peaks high and remote. But up in these meadows, with the peaks close at hand, it's the forest that pales.

Above: lakes at the head of Excelsior Creek, seen along the Skyline Trail in Jasper National Park, Alberta. Rocky summit in the background is the Watchtower (9157'/2791 m)

*Above: **gray wolf** (Canis lupus)*

A hunter in the willows

Pictured is a typical gray wolf. This one is, indeed, gray, but in the Canadian Rockies wolves can come in other colors—black, white, brown, combinations—and sometimes it's hard to tell if you're looking at a real wolf or somebody's dog.

The eyes usually tell the tale. The eyes of wild canids are bright yellow, while the eyes of malamutes and other wolf-like dogs are usually brown or blue.

Not so many years ago, wolves weren't wanted anywhere in the Rockies, not even in the national parks, where they were killed as vermin. South of Jasper National Park they were exterminated. Nowadays we know better; the wolf has its place in the ecosystem—its job is to eat hoofed animals, of which there would otherwise be too many—and *Canis lupus* is making a

justified comeback. Packs are now present in all the national parks, including Waterton-Glacier.

Given that fact, please be reassured that wolves are not dangerous to humans. Little Red Riding Hood has given wolves a bad rap, as have countless other folk tales. Careful research has shown that not a single death in North America can be attributed unequivocally to a wolf, and there have been fewer than half a dozen injuries. Domestic dogs are much more dangerous. Even coyotes are more dangerous *(see page 65)*. Why wolves are so respectful of humans is anyone's guess; they just avoid us as much as possible. If you see one, consider yourself lucky. You have been honored by one of the world's great hunters.

Maligne Lake—as seen by the few

To get this view, you have to ski or snowshoe three miles (5 km) from the end of the road. It's a steady uphill plod through the trees, with little inspiring scenery along the way, but eventually you come over a rise and there it is: Maligne Lake, stretching like a white ribbon 13.8 miles (22.3 km) into the wilderness.

Maligne is the longest natural lake in the Canadian Rockies; even this view doesn't reach quite to the end. In summer, visitors ride down the lake in large, noisy cruise boats. They disembark, troop over to a viewpoint, take photos and ride back. In winter the ice is thick, the boats are gone and the silence is sublime.

So is the cross-country skiing up here.

The duck that braves the rapids

Small and plump, this harlequin duck looks more suited to waddling around the edge of a garden pond than doing what it does: diving into whitewater rivers and scooting along the bouldery bottom in search of aquatic insects to eat. Birders refer to this species as a "torrent duck," which seems apt; it winters on the west coast, among the breakers, and it spends the summers in the roughest inland water it can find. The picture shows the male harlequin. Females are plain brown, with white patches on the head.

The males arrive in the Rockies in May, stay for only a few weeks (long enough to mate with the females), then return to the coast—leaving the duckling-rearing to the females.

Above left: in the background, highest on the horizon, is Samson Peak (10,108'/3081 m). Maligne Valley, Jasper National Park, Alberta

Above: harlequin duck (Histrionicus histrionicus)

The forest floor

North-facing slopes in the Canadian Rockies are cooler and wetter than south-facing slopes, because at this latitude the sun strikes north-facing slopes at a gentle angle. In winter the sun can't reach such exposures at all, so the snow piles up deeply there. Such a microclimate provides plenty of moisture and not much direct sunlight—a fine environment for feather mosses: the large, very frilly moss species seen in the photo. Emerging from the feather-moss carpet are a small blueberry plant and a bolete mushroom.

Cardboard cutouts

Given a bright sunset like this one, the peaks below lose their third dimension in the extreme contrast between darkness and light. The ridges extending toward the viewer disappear in shadow; the intervening valleys fade away. Everything becomes as flat as a paper silhouette. Summer sunsets last a long time in the Canadian Rockies, and so does this effect.

Above: view west to the Colin Range in central Jasper National Park, Alberta

Young, but already fierce

This fledgling great horned owl is just starting to grow the feather tufts (the "horns") that characterize its species. Having recently left the nest, it is experimenting with prey: discovering which are easiest to catch, which bite back as the talons plunge in, and so on. When this bird was a nestling, hatched in late winter, its parents probably fed it on a diet guaranteed to produce a tough youngster: skunk. When it grows up, this owl will let its voice float through the night woods, "Hoo, hoo-oo-oo, hoo, hoo." Small furry creatures will shiver when they hear it.

The lake that isn't a lake

Jasper Lake is big, and thus it ought to be deep, but it's shallow—so shallow that you can stroll out to the middle of it without getting your knees wet. In a normal lake the flow of water is undetectably slow; in Jasper Lake you can feel the current passing around your legs. This is a moving sheet of water, not a lake. What we have here is a flood.

There is an annual cycle. Every summer the Athabasca River swells with meltwater and backs up behind a narrow spot at the far end of the picture. Jasper Lake appears. In autumn the flow diminishes and the lake dribbles away, back into the main river channel.

Left behind is the empty basin of Jasper Lake, wide and sandy. All winter the wind howls down this valley—it's a major valley, cutting through the front ranges of the Rockies—and the wind carries the sand along, each grain hopping and skipping eastward until it hits a particular spot where the alignment of the peaks limits the wind speed. Here the sand stops, piling up to form something unexpected in the Canadian Rockies: dunes.

Above: looking northeast down Jasper Lake toward the Bosche Range (left), Boule Range (center) and Miette Range (right). View from Highway 16, Jasper National Park, Alberta

Left: great horned owl (Bubo virginianus)

117

Beware of the devil's club

The ferns are no problem, but that large-leaved plant certainly is. The stems, branches and even the undersides of the leaves are all armed with sharp spines, giving this species its evil-sounding name: devil's-club. For once, the scientific name, too, suits it perfectly: *Oplopanax horridum*.

Devil's-club is rare in the Canadian Rockies, limited to a few unusually wet spots on the western slope. Never mind the devil's-club; such places are worth visiting because they are very beautiful. The trees—western redcedar, Douglas-fir, western hemlock—are big, and they grow thickly, diffusing the sunlight and providing homes for shade-loving mushrooms, red-berried mountain ash, twining honeysuckle and a pretty white wildflower called Nancy-over-the-ground. None of these species grows elsewhere in the Rockies, but they are common in Columbian forest, the ecologist's name for this ecosystem.

Interested? You can stroll through the excellent example shown here on the Kinney Lake Trail in Mount Robson Provincial Park.

Above: Kinney Lake Trail,
Mount Robson Provincial Park

Highest peak in the Canadian Rockies

Mt. Robson stands head and shoulders above any of its neighbors. This backcountry view shows the north side of the mountain, with two famous features: glacially colored Berg Lake, looking like liquid turquoise, and the Tumbling Glacier (the one on the left), which contributes the icebergs.

The Tumbling Glacier is often called "Berg Glacier" by mistake. Perhaps the geographers should give up and rename it Berg Glacier officially, because there is another Tumbling Glacier elsewhere in the Rockies (in Kootenay National Park).

Mist Glacier, on the right, lies under the Emperor Face of Mt. Robson, the highest cliff in the Canadian Rockies: 7600 feet (2315 m) from the lake to the top. At 12,972' (3954 m), Robson is not the highest peak in the Rocky Mountains; Colorado's Mt. Elbert (14,433'/4399 m) is higher. But Robson is the *biggest* peak in the Rockies, American or Canadian, because it rises over 10,000 vertical feet (3000 m) above its base. Runner-up is Pikes Peak, which rises 7500 feet (2300 m) above Colorado Springs.

The origin of Mt. Robson's name is a mystery, but it may refer to a fur-trade figure of the early 1800s named "Robinson." The Indian name is perhaps more appropriate: "Yuh-Hai-Has-Kun," translated as "The Mountain of the Spiral Road to Heaven." It's a difficult road; Mt. Robson attracts climbers from all over the world, and most of them turn back before reaching the summit.

Above: the skyline, from left to right: Resplendent Mountain, (11,240'/3426 m), Mt. Waffl (9482'/2890 m), The Helmet (11,220'/3420 m) and Mt. Robson (12,972'/3954 m). View from meadows above Toboggan Falls, Mount Robson Provincial Park, British Columbia

Above: common loon (Gavia immer)

Big country, small creature

With the front ranges fading to evening blue behind it, a solitary loon goes about its business on Rock Lake. Does it ever think about the scale of its surroundings? Does it care? What is a single sentient creature worth, in comparison to hundreds of cold stone peaks? What is a human being worth? These are the kinds of questions that come to mind in a place like this. It makes us feel small.

Left: view west across Rock Lake,
Willmore Wilderness Park, Alberta

121

Above: fireweed (Epilobium angustifolium)

Parting thoughts

As the human tide floods the globe, we need every island of wilderness we have left. The Canadian Rockies are such an island, and it's a large one. We have to keep these mountains unspoiled, which means we have to keep them wild.

So here is an invitation to do your bit. It's simple: take the mountains on their terms, not civilization's terms. Better the tent than the hotel; better the hiking boot than the automobile. Where there are no buildings, no roads and no motors, there you will find wilderness. It's really as simple as that.

The Canadian Rockies wilderness is easy to get to. It's not like Patagonia or the Galapagos. Banff National Park is in central North America. Jetports are near; highways cut right across the mountains at five points. Travelling to the trailheads is easy.

All the more reason for not letting it get any easier. Have you noticed that most of the pictures in this book were taken in national and provincial parks? That's where the wilderness is least compromised. That's where the animals live. That's where there are the fewest roads.

Let's keep it that way. Let's make sure that our legislators know that those parks are not here to produce profits. This could wreck them in one generation. The parks are here to last forever, handed down intact to every generation. A sign posted by the Canadian parks service in Jasper a few years ago said it perfectly:

Parks Canada is not the owner, but rather the trustee of a national inheritance that must never be spent.

❏

John Winnie

Paul Lally

Ben Gadd

About the Photographers

John Winnie is a Montana-based nature photographer who lives beside a lake in the northwest mountains of the state. John grew up exploring the Rockies, working at Glacier National Park while studying zoology at the University of Montana. He continues to spend all his available time outdoors, hiking, studying and photographing the mountains. His photographs have appeared in books and magazines, as well as on posters.

Paul Lally has traveled throughout North America shooting landscape and closeup photographs, but especially wildlife, his favorite subject. Paul's interest in wilderness travel is evident from the many pictures in this book that were taken while snowshoeing, hiking, backpacking, or mountain biking. His photographs have been published in many calendars and magazines, and also exhibited in art shows and galleries.

About the Author

Ben Gadd is a freelance interpretive guide in Jasper National Park, a job he describes as "rent-a-naturalist." Trained as a geologist, Ben has broadened his interests and built a career in natural history. The author of *Handbook of the Canadian Rockies* and two other books, he is a recognized authority on the region. When not teaching or writing, he hikes, climbs and cross-country skis in the mountains he loves best.

Photo Credits

Paul Lally

John Winnie

Acknowledgments

I would like to thank my families.

John Winnie

I would like to thank the following for their assistance and/or contributions to this project: Sherpa Inc., Chicago, IL; Schwinn Bicycle C., Chicago, IL; Wheatons, Kalispell, MT; A special thanks to everyone at Photo Video Plus, Kalispell, MT; The North Face (especially Lynden Hynes for her more than gracious assistance), Berkeley, CA; The staff at the information center for parks Canada and BC Parks. A note to Brian Patton, "the *Trail Guide to the Canadian Rockies* was indispensible." Thank you Tom & Betty Reed for sharing your warm hospitality. Most of all I would like to thank our publishers Ted & Beverly Paul for giving us the opportunity.

Paul Lally